LOVE IS A
KITTEN

summersdale

LOVE IS A KITTEN

An Hachette UK Company
www.hachette.co.uk

Summersdale Publishers Ltd
Part of Octopus Publishing Group Limited
Carmelite House
50 Victoria Embankment
LONDON
EC4Y 0DZ
UK

www.summersdale.com

Printed and bound in China

ISBN: 978-1-78783-262-6

Substantial discounts on bulk quantities of Summersdale books are available to corporations, professional associations and other organizations. For details contact general enquiries: telephone: +44 (0) 1243 771107 or email: enquiries@summersdale.com.

❤ INTRODUCTION ❤

Is there anything on earth quite as adorable as a kitten? Those big round eyes. Those tiny mews. Those wobbly steps on little paws. What they lack in size, they make up for in personality, and it's hard to believe that anybody could be immune to their fluffy, frolicking charms. If these heart-melting bundles of fur have got you head over heels in love, dive into this paw-some little book – a celebration of our tiniest feline friends, which will prove that a kitten really is the purr-fect companion.

ALL YOU NEED
♥ IS LOVE... ♥

AND A KITTEN

THERE ARE FEW THINGS IN LIFE
MORE HEART-WARMING THAN
TO BE WELCOMED BY A CAT.

Tay Hohoff

IT'S EXHAUSTING
♥ BEING THIS CUTE ♥

ALL THE TIME

ANIMALS ARE SUCH AGREEABLE
FRIENDS — THEY ASK NO QUESTIONS,
THEY PASS NO CRITICISMS.

George Eliot

ARE YOU
♥ KITTEN ME ♥

RIGHT NOW?

THERE ARE TWO MEANS OF
REFUGE FROM THE MISERY
OF LIFE: MUSIC AND CATS.

Albert Schweitzer

WHEN I GROW UP,

♥ I'M GOING TO BE ♥

PURR-FECT

IF THERE WERE TO BE A UNIVERSAL
SOUND DEPICTING PEACE, I WOULD
SURELY VOTE FOR THE PURR.

Barbara L. Diamond

TAKE A

❤ MOMENT TO ❤

PAWS

IN NINE LIFETIMES, YOU'LL NEVER
KNOW AS MUCH ABOUT YOUR CAT
AS YOUR CAT KNOWS ABOUT YOU.

Michel de Montaigne

WHAT DO

♥ YOU MEAN, ♥

"YOUR CHAIR"?

YOU CAN'T LOOK AT A SLEEPING CAT AND FEEL TENSE.

Jane Pauley

IT'S ME —
I'M THE CAT
♥ THAT GOT ♥

THE CREAM

THE IDEAL OF CALM EXISTS IN A SITTING CAT.

Jules Renard

♥ THE SNUG LIFE ♥

CHOSE ME

I HAVE STUDIED MANY PHILOSOPHERS AND MANY CATS. THE WISDOM OF CATS IS INFINITELY SUPERIOR.

Hippolyte Taine

YOU MAY ADDRESS

♥ ME AS ♥

"YOUR HIGHNESS"

YOU WILL ALWAYS BE LUCKY
IF YOU KNOW HOW TO MAKE
FRIENDS WITH STRANGE CATS.

Proverb

I'M MAJESTIC

♥ AND I ♥

KNOW IT

UNTIL ONE HAS LOVED
AN ANIMAL, A PART OF ONE'S
SOUL REMAINS UNAWAKENED.

Anatole France

LIFE IS BETTER WITH

♥ A KITTEN ♥

(OR TWO)

AN ANIMAL'S EYES HAVE THE POWER TO SPEAK A GREAT LANGUAGE.

Martin Buber

♥ TODAY I'M ♥

FELINE FINE

ONE SMALL CAT CHANGES
COMING HOME TO AN EMPTY
HOUSE TO COMING HOME.

Pam Brown

WARNING: I'M CUTE ♥ BUT DEADLY. ♥

NO, SERIOUSLY!

WHEN THEY ARE AMONG US, CATS ARE ANGELS.

George Sand

♥ LITTLE PAWS, ♥

BIG DREAMS

I LOVE CATS BECAUSE I ENJOY MY
HOME; AND, LITTLE BY LITTLE,
THEY BECOME ITS VISIBLE SOUL.

Jean Cocteau

FAST, FURIOUS,

♥ FEARLESS, ♥

FLUFFY

ONE CAT JUST LEADS TO ANOTHER.

Ernest Hemingway

♥ CHECK ♥

MEOW-T

THERE IS NO MORE INTREPID EXPLORER THAN A KITTEN.

Champfleury

MY HOBBIES INCLUDE
FROLICKING
♥ AND BEING ♥
_____

ADORABLE
_____

I BELIEVE CATS TO BE SPIRITS COME TO EARTH.

Jules Verne

LOOK DEEP INTO
MY EYES... YOU
♥ FEEL COMPELLED TO ♥

FEED ME TUNA

WHAT GREATER GIFT THAN THE LOVE OF A CAT.

Charles Dickens

I NEVER MET

♥ A BOX I ♥

DIDN'T LIKE

IT IS DIFFICULT TO OBTAIN
THE FRIENDSHIP OF A CAT. IT
IS A PHILOSOPHICAL ANIMAL...
ONE THAT DOES NOT PLACE ITS
AFFECTIONS THOUGHTLESSLY.

Théophile Gautier

EVEN THE
FIERCEST WARRIORS
♥ GET SLEEPY ♥
SOMETIMES

THE SMALLEST FELINE IS A MASTERPIECE.

Leonardo da Vinci

♥ PAW-SOME ♥
_____

SQUAD
_____

CATS ARE CONNOISSEURS OF COMFORT.

James Herriot

♥ THEY CALL ME ♥

WOOL-VERINE

I HAVE LIVED WITH SEVERAL ZEN MASTERS — ALL OF THEM CATS.

Eckhart Tolle

IT'S ALWAYS
A GOOD DAY
♥ TO BE A ♥
KITTEN

MY CAT IS MY LITTLE
SOULMATE. HE'S NOT JUST
A CAT, HE'S MY FRIEND.

Tracey Emin

If you're interested in finding out more about our books, find us on Facebook at **Summersdale Publishers** and follow us on Twitter at **@Summersdale**.

www.summersdale.com

IMAGE CREDITS